How to use this book

Follow the advice, in italics, given for you on each page.
Support the children as they read the text that is shaded in cream.
***Praise** the children at every step!*

Detailed guidance is provided in the Read Write Inc. Phonics Handbook

9 reading activities

Children:

Practise reading the speed sounds.

Read the green, red and challenge words for the story.

Listen as you read the introduction.

Discuss the vocabulary check with you.

Read the story.

Re-read the story and discuss the 'questions to talk about'.

Read the story with fluency and expression.

Answer the questions to 'read and answer'.

Practise reading the speed words.

Speed sounds

Vowels *Say the sounds in and out of order.*

a	e	i	o	u	ay	ee	igh	ow
	ea				a-e	ea	i-e	o-e
					a	e	i	oa
					ai	y	y	o
					aigh			

oo	oo	ar	or	air	ir	ou	oy	ire	ear
u-e			oor	are	ur	ow	oi		
ue			ore		er				
ew			aw						

*Each box contains one sound but sometimes more than one grapheme. Focus graphemes are **circled**.*

Green words

Read in Fred Talk (pure sounds).

dear year hear ear smear fear

hire fire

Read in syllables.

vamp\`ire fire\`work bon\`fire en\`tire re\`quire

en\`quire tire\`some

Read the root word first and then with the ending.

tear → tears

clear → cleared

appear → appeared

disappear → disappeared → disappearing

wire → wired

retire → retired

tire → tired

near → nearly

Red words

walk said they were was what small are

any here son who would there

Challenge word

eyes

Dear Vampire

Introduction

What makes a good party?

If you were going to have a bonfire party, what would you have?

Do you remember Wailing Winny and her car boot sale? She is planning a bonfire party and decides to hire a scary vampire to entertain her guests. But the vampire who turns up isn't what she expected. It's a vampire bat - and an old one at that.

Will her party still be a success?

Story written by Gill Munton
Illustrated by Tim Archbold

Vocabulary check

Discuss the meaning (as used in the story) after the children have read each word.

	definition:	sentence/phrase:
require	*need*	*I require a top vampire for my bonfire party.*
fangs	*sharp, pointy teeth*	*You must have sharp fangs.*
retired	*given up work - because of old age*	*I'm retired, really.*
tiresome	*boring, irritating*	*You must do something about these tiresome cobwebs.*
drooped	*flopped down*	*The vampire drooped sadly from the lampshade.*
hopeless	*useless, rubbish*	*You're a hopeless vampire.*

Punctuation to note in this story:

1. Capital letters to start sentences and full stops to end sentences

2. Capital letters for names

3. Exclamation marks to show anger, shock and surprise

4. 'Wait and see' dots...

5. Speech marks

He flapped up to Smelly Nelly,

who was dancing with her eyes shut,

and brushed his little wings against her face.

But Nelly only said, "You must do something

about these tiresome cobwebs, Winny."

Next, he perched on Dustbin Dave's ear

and sank his gums into his neck.

But Dave only said, "My collar must be too tight.

It's pinching me!"

The vampire drooped sadly from the lampshade.

"Never mind!" whispered Phantom Phil. "Have a drink. Fresh blood for you, is it?"

"Fangs very much," said the vampire, taking a sip.

But when he saw Phil, he was nearly in tears.

He cleared his throat, and wiped a smear

of blood from his nose.

"I'm scared of ghosts!" he squeaked.

"You toothless twit!" wailed Winny.

"That's my husband, Phantom Phil. You've got nothing to fear from him!"

Sam Spook appeared next, carrying a tray of spiders on sticks.

The vampire nearly fainted.

"I'm getting tired of this!" wailed Winny.

"You're a hopeless vampire! Just... go away!"

"Be careful, Winny," said Phil, "and put that wand down!"

There was a bang, and a flash – and then, nothing. The vampire had disappeared!

"Never mind!" grinned Winny. "Who needs vampires for a good party?"

and they danced and sang until dawn.

Questions to talk about

Re-read the page. Read the question to the children. Tell them whether it is a **FIND IT** *question or* **PROVE IT** *question.*

FIND IT

- ✓ *Turn to the page*
- ✓ *Read the question*
- ✓ *Find the answer*

PROVE IT

- ✓ *Turn to the page*
- ✓ *Read the question*
- ✓ *Find your evidence*
- ✓ *Explain why*

Page 9:	FIND IT	*What type of party is Wailing Winny having?*
Page 10:	PROVE IT	*Who does Winnie email?*
Page 11:	FIND IT	*What kind of vampire actually comes to the party?*
Page 12:	PROVE IT	*What does Winny think of the vampire bat?*
Page 13:	PROVE IT	*Why isn't the bat very scary?*
Page 14:	PROVE IT	*Who is the vampire bat scared of? Why?*
Page 15:	PROVE IT	*How does Winny get rid of the vampire?*

Questions to read and answer

(Children complete without your help.)

1. Why did Winny want a vampire?

2. Winny wanted a scary vampire.

   What was different about the vampire that came?

3. Why did Dave say 'My collar must be too tight. It's pinching me!'?

4. Why was the vampire scared of Phantom Phil?

5. What did Winny do to the vampire?

Speed words

Children practise reading the words across the rows, down the columns and in and out of order clearly and quickly.

wrote	careful	dancing	furry	face
whispered	fire	vampire	bonfire	retired
tiresome	require	walk	son	who
would	there	bought	buy	watch